ONE DAY CROCHET MASTERY

The Complete Beginner's Guide to Learn Crochet in Under 1 Day!

10 Step by Step Projects That Inspire You – Images Included

By Ellen Warren

© *Copyright 2015*

All rights reserved. No part of this book may be reproduced or transmitted in any form or by any means, electronically or mechanically, including photocopy, recording, or by and information storage or retrieval system, without the written permission from the publisher, except in the case of brief quotations embodied in critical articles or reviews.

Trademarks are the property of their respective holders. When used, trademarks are for the benefit of the trademark owner only.

DISCLAIMER

The information provided herein is stated to be truthful and consistent, in that any liability, in terms of inattention or otherwise, by any usage or abusage of any policies, processes, or directions contained within is the solitary and utter responsibility of the recipient reader. Under no circumstances will any legal responsibility or blame be held against the publisher for any reparation, damages, or monetary loss due to the information herein, either directly or indirectly. Respective authors hold all rights not held by publisher.

Note from the Author:

Welcome to the amazing world of Crochet! As some of you know from my other books, this has been a passion of mine for more than 15 years, and I'm thrilled that you will allow me to help you learn this beautiful art form. The purpose of the book is to teach you the basics of crochet stitches and patterns. With this book and a bit of patience, you will be able to create beautiful, interesting and useful products that are real pieces of art.

Crochet is such a part of our everyday life, that we take it for granted! This book for beginners is designed to give you an introduction to the art, and give you the toolbox to develop basic designs and progress to more complex and decorative projects. Once you read this book, and complete some of the suggested projects, you'll be well on your way to having both the skills and the confidence necessary to start trying your hand at a vast number of different crochet projects. The peculiarity and beauty of this system is that you don't need any previous experience or knowledge about crochet. This book is a complete step-by-step guide to help you get started. All the needed information will be given to you; from choosing your crochet hook to finishing off a beautiful rainbow coloured bag for a sunny day.

Nowadays, crocheting and knitting are extremely popular and in fashion. "Yarn bombing" or "urban knitting" is a new way to express art using knitting or crocheting to decorate towns. Many celebrities are now practicing knitting or crocheting (or both), and there are bars and pubs all over the world dedicated to people passionate about this hobby.

This book will guide you through what you need to know to get started on this very traditional craft that will last you for a lifetime. You will see that in a couple of years, you will have a large collection of patterns to share with family and friends.

Let's get started!!

       Ellen Warren

Chapter Index

Learn to Choose Your Supplies & Tools 8
    The correct hooks for a beginner 8
    Choosing suitable yarn 14
    Wools to avoid 15

Learn How to Hold the Hook & Yarn 21
    Forefinger method 22
    Little finger method 25
    Making a chain 27

Basic Crochet Stitches for Beginners 31
    Single crochet 31
    Double crochet 34
    Treble Crochet 35

Learn to Crochet a Granny Square 40

Add Stitches of Interest 50
    Working a scallop border 50
    Make a loop and work 30 chains 52

Using Different Stitches to Their Best Advantages 56
    Decreasing and increasing 57
    Edging work 59

Trying your hand at using crochet cotton 60

Glossary of crochet abbreviations 61

Classic and Less Common Crocheted Artefacts 63

Fashion on the Catwalks and in Shopping Centers 68

Early Origins and History 72

Beginner's Designs Tutorial 79

   Baby Bib 79

   Little Turtle 83

   Snowflakes 89

Crochet Potholder (Single Crochet) 95

   Little fish for children 107

   A Stand for the cup 115

   Little Angel 120

Conclusion 128

   **** PREVIEW OTHER BOOKS BY THIS AUTHOR****
.... 130

Learn to Choose Your Supplies & Tools

To begin learning to crochet, you will need to gather the necessary materials. It is quite important to choose your tools properly in the beginning. You do not want to get bored and stop your practice only because you chose something too difficult. This book is based on extensive experience and will guide you in choosing and selecting the materials suited for beginners. Experience has shown that not all yarns are the same — some are difficult to work with little or no skill at all and others are more beginner-friendly. What a beginner needs to really get the feeling for the craft are yarns with proper thickness plus particular sizes of crochet hooks.

The correct hooks for a beginner
In order to clearly see the stitches while you are working, you will need a relatively big crochet hook. You will work with wool in the beginning, as it is the most suitable material to start with. Later,

you will try cotton and other materials. Besides, wool is the material used for many projects. It is a good idea to master wool very well before trying something else.

To find the perfect crocket hook for your hand and your style may take some time. Now, as a beginner, do not think too much about it — finding hooks to make your work easier is enough. What you have to avoid is buying crocket hooks made out of plastic or bamboo because these are not easy to use. Bamboo ones are often inexpensive, made from natural material, and definitely cool. Plastic ones have wonderful color patterns. The problem is that the wool tends to get stuck on them and creates problems you do not need to have at your early stage. The best idea is to buy a plastic coated metal hook — not so fashionable, but easier to use for sure. Neutral and light colors are strongly suggested. Multi-color hooks can confuse you while you are crocheting.

Simple plastic coated crochet hook

Later, as you get more experienced and you start to use cotton too, metal crochet hooks are ideal. Of course, you will build up a wonderful collection of every kind of crochet hooks with time.

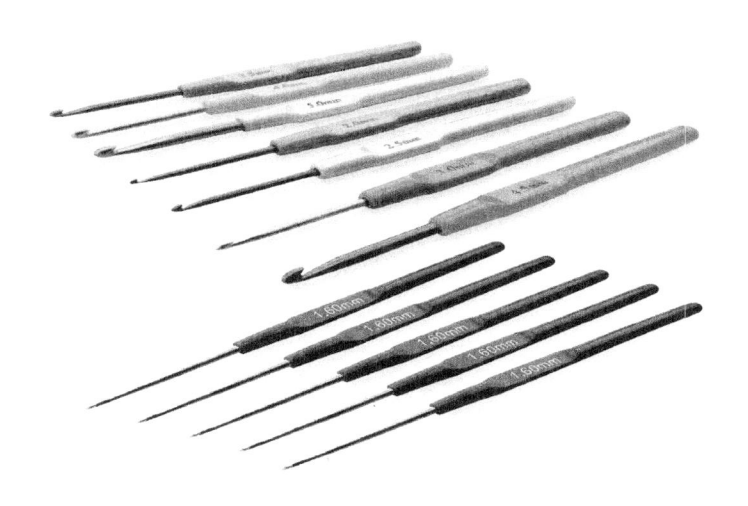

Wonderful metal ergonomic crocheting hooks set

For the best size for beginners, we have to consider that they differ depending on the country and the brand of hook. In the USA, the size that you need will be either a G6 or an H8 (better to have both) which is the European equivalent of 6 and 8. It is better to buy different sizes to start your new crochet experience. In this case, the advice of your favorite shop keeper will be very useful. The size depends on what you want to create. The size of the hook and the yarn you use determine the size of the item being crocheted. This is very similar to using various knitting needles. Thus, if you want a bigger square, you have to adjust the needle accordingly. Dimensions of the hooks become even more important if you want to use scrap wool and one is thicker than the rest. To get the stitches even, you just use a smaller sized hook for the thicker wool so that the stitches all look the same size.

Crochet Hook Sizes

Old UK	Metric	US
000	10.0mm	
00	9.00mm	
0	8.00mm	
2	7.00mm	K-10 1/2
3	6.50mm	10 1/4
4	6.00mm	J-10
5	5.50mm	I-9
6	5.00mm	H-8
7	4.50mm	7
8	4.00mm	G-6
9	3.75mm	F-5
9	3.50mm	E-4
10	3.25mm	D-3
12	2.75mm	C-2
13	2.25mm	B-1
14	2.00mm	B-1
15	1.75mm	5 steel
16	1.50mm	7 steel
17	1.25mm	8 steel
18	1.00mm	10 steel

Here is an example of an "old" UK to USA crochet hook conversion chart.

Choosing suitable yarn

During your shopping trip, you will be attracted to and tempted by some beautiful multi-colored yarns you can buy. Forget about it for now. At this stage, what you really need is a pale-colored yarn so you can see the processes that make up the stitches. You can choose many colors but avoid very dark ones. Of course, later you will be able to express your creativity by choosing the weirdest yarn in the world or whatever is suited to work on your ideas and to what you are making. As a beginner, you should stick to a simple yarn — not too textured and definitely not a "hairy" one. Avoid specialty yarn at this stage. The thickness should be a worsted weight or double knitting equivalent. They are easy to hold, so you will be able to avoid unnecessary problems.

Here is an example of perfect worsted wool type for crochet. Do not choose wool darker than the blue one on the right.

Wools to avoid

Do not try to crochet with wool that is bumpy or has a texture that makes it difficult to make the work even. It's the same old story — you need to start with the easiest way and, step by step, you will able to use any type of wool when you've developed your skill enough. The main problem with textured wool is that when the hook gets caught in the uneven feature, it can be very confusing for a beginner to see what they have done wrong. The stitch formation will be unclear and it will be difficult to go back and fix your mistake.

These are samples of specialty yarns that you should avoid.

The basic equipment is quite simple — you will need a small pair of scissors and a knitting basket to keep loose balls of wool in. One of the qualities of crochet is that it is the best way to use scrap wool. Get a pair of your favorite colors for learning with, and when you finish, you can put them away for your next training.

You will also need a darning needle for items that need to be stitched together. With that, you are ready to start.

In the next chapter, we will start to talk about practice. Analyze the different stitches one at a time and see the kinds of projects that can be made using those stitches. We will start with understanding how to hold your crochet hook and wool. This will develop into showing you the whole process of creating stitches. You will develop your style and use your fingers in your way with time.

In crochet, a combination of basic stitches usually makes up the patterns, but the basic is all you need to know to make items such as granny squares. Granny squares are what you really need to begin with. They are versatile, simple to work with, and can be made into a huge variety of different items.

It is a good idea to ask to your wool shop for a simple crochet pattern when you are actually ready to start. You will notice how crochet patterns minimize all of the stitches that you are being shown during these learning stages. As usual, it is recommended for you not to try anything too complex at this stage. When you buy a pattern, tell the assistant in the store that you are a beginner and you do not want to start with anything too complex.

At the end of this book, you will find a list of abbreviations that will be quite useful to decipher patterns and this can be added to as you learn new stitches. Check the instructions in potential patterns. What you want are those using fundamental stitches: single crochet, double crochet, chains, clusters, and trebles. You will find many patterns available for small items. For example, you can create a series of small items such as "amigurumi". They are easy to make and can be used for every kind of holiday decorations. Amigurumi are knitted or crocheted stuffed toys, coming from the Japanese art of knitting, and you need to master the single crochet stitch. Simple patterns can be found easily on the web, so your research needs just a few clicks.

Simple Christmas decoration

Amigurumi

Learn How to Hold the Hook & Yarn

There are many ways to hold the crochet hook. The "simplest" way or the "best" way does not really exist. What you need is the best way for you, your hands, and your comfort. To hold the crochet hook itself is not difficult because of the design. The central area is flat so you can hold the hook without the risk of it turning around during the process of using it. You will have a firm grip on it and the hook will always face the right way for the next stitch.

What you want to grasp is how to wind the wool around your finger. One of the most important things to master in crocheting is how to uniformly control the tension between the wool and the work. Once you control the tension and know how to deal with hooks and yarn, you are halfway to mastering crocheting already. There are some simple ways to do it. The most used method by experts is the forefinger hold technique. In this technique, you will use mainly the forefinger (index).

Forefinger method

Step one. With your palm facing downwards, bring the tail end of the yarn up through your little finger and index finger.

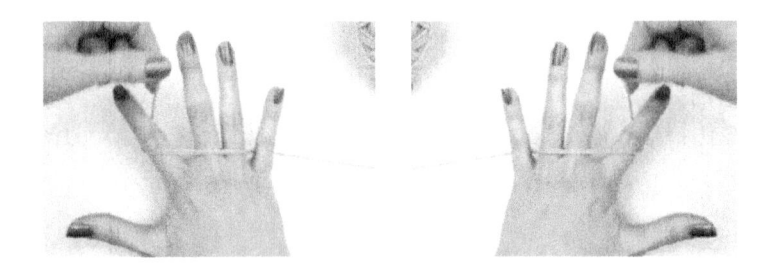

Step one

Step two. Continue to bring the yarn over the top of your hand, looping it around your forefinger.

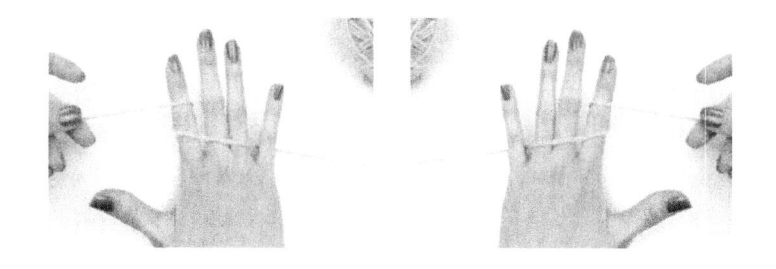

Step two

You main hand is always the one that holds the hook. So if you are left-handed, it will be the left. The images above show the left and right hand ways for holding yarn.

The image below (picture 1) shows what you want to reach. Hold the hook firmly, then make a loop in the end of the yarn. Pass this loop over the crochet hook as the starting point.

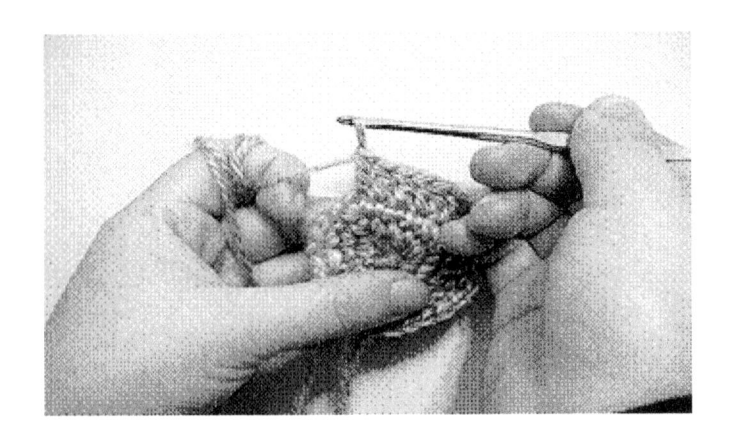

Picture 1

If, for some reason you do not want to (or cannot) use your forefinger, there is another way to hold the yarn using your little finger. Remember that you need to maximize your comfort.

When you find the best way for you, it will follow you for a lifetime. It is better to spend time in the beginning finding it than discover the "perfect" one for you later. By the way, if you start to cramp up when you are using the style you like, stop using that style (even if is your favorite) and try something different. Your own body is sending to you a warning — listen to it.

Little finger method

Step one. With your palm facing downwards (as it always will be when you start holding your yarn), bring the tail end of your yarn up between your little finger and ring finger.

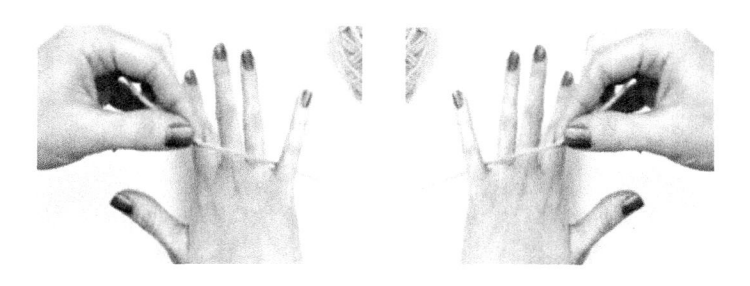

Step one

Step two. Form a loop around your little finger and bring the tail end over the top of your hand.

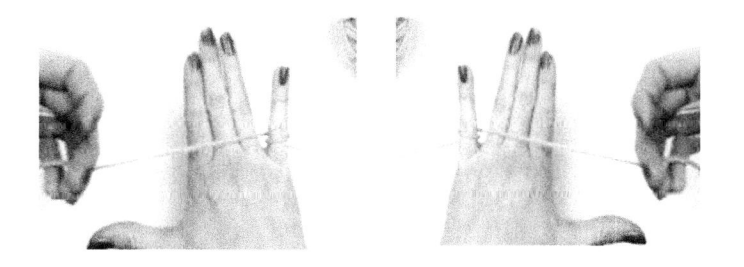

Step two

Step three. Use the thumb and forefinger to grip the yarn for control. Please bear in mind that the concept is the same for every holding yarn technique: to control the tension and keep it even.

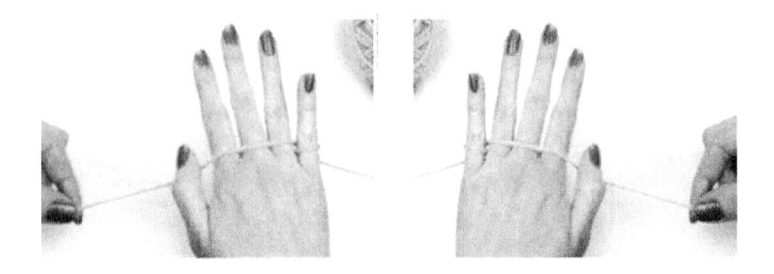

Step three

Those holds are the basic ones. According to experts, the most used and comfortable are less painful to use for long periods of time. Of course, there are hundreds of tutorials to research on the web once you've had more experience. But for now, it's not recommended to browse too much. Use the basics and be confident with it for a while to avoid being disappointed or worse, get bored.

Now we have our hook firm in our hand, our yarn

under control. It's time to start to make something.

Making a chain

Wherever you look, whoever you ask about starting your crochet career, the answer will be the same — the very base of your crochet is the chain (picture 2) and almost every crochet pattern begins with a chain. If working in rounds or working granny squares, you need to make five chains in a row and join them so that you create a circle. All subsequent squares will be worked in that circle to start shaping your crochet.

How do you create a chain? First you have to form a slip knot (picture 3). In most crochet projects, the first step is making the slip knot. Again, when it comes to slip knots, there are many ways to create it. We will examine one of the easiest way. First, twist a loose loop of yarn onto the hook. Hold the tail of the yarn between your thumb and index finger. Use the rest of your fingers to control the yarn that keeps unwinding from the ball. Draw the yarn into the loop with your crochet hook. Tighten the loose slip knot that is now on your hook. Remember not to tighten it too much. Make sure your crochet hook can move easily in the loop. Now, start the chain to make progress.

You have your slip knot with a hook, now wrap the yarn over the loop and pull it through to make a new loop. You have made your first chain stitch. In order to make more chain stitches, make another loop and draw the yarn through. You can repeat this as much is needed for your project.

When you have five chains, you can join them to form a circle. As we said before, all the stitches will be worked in that circle. Once the chain is done, you need to join the circle. This is done by putting the crochet hook through the first stitch, the wool around the hook, and pulling it through. This leaves you ready to commence with the first row.

Picture 2

There is no point to change colors at this stage. You are doing your first chain, your first circle. It's better to try more difficult experimentations with color later. But if you really want to change colors, you have to cut the wool and pull it through the final loop so that it is tightly fastened. However, by following the guide step by step with the stitches, you'll need to keep the wool attached, so you will not be able to change colors. We will go through this topic later in the granny square section (chapter 4).

Now you learned the basics — holding your crochet hook and making a chain and a circle to work with. You can increase the number of chains as much as you want to make a larger circle if you want to or need to. When working on a flat item, opposed to one that is worked in rounds, you will need to work across instead of into a circle, thus building your crochet work. Working across a chain is dealt later in the book. How to make a sweater? Merely continue by adding rows, keeping the sides as straight as possible until shaping is required. Now it is time to learn different types of stitches in the next chapter.

Basic Crochet Stitches for Beginners

Having learned how to make a chain, now it's important to understand that the chain is not used only as casting on, but it is also used to create shapes or the corners for granny squares. By the end of this guide, you will have learned how to use chains for those purposes. Now we will take a deep look into the ways to create different stitches and the most common stitches in crochet, giving you the ability to work from patterns.

Single crochet

The single crochet is the most commonly found stitch and the easiest to make. Easy and fast, it is good for creating shaped items like jackets or skirts. It is also good for decorating finished work as it creates a tight and dense fabric. You can use this stitch alone over and over again or together with other stitches. It is definitely the most fundamental of all stitches.

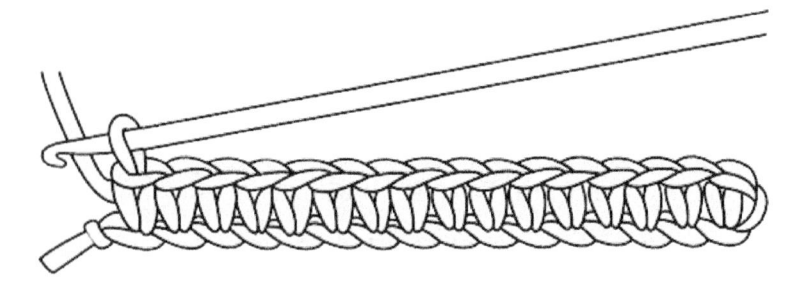

Final result

How to do it?

Step one. First of all, prepare a series of chains, then insert your hook on the SECOND chain facing you and your yarn.

Step two. Wrap the yarn towards to you with your hook hand. Remember to wrap it from back to front (wrap the yarn from the back to the front — this is called "yarn over" or YO). At this point, pull the hook. If all have been done properly, you are supposed to have two loops to work with.

Step three. Pass the yarn through the two loops. You've completed your first single crochet. Repeat the operation until you finish all the chains. To continue, put your hook onto the next chain stitch and repeat all the operations from step two to complete the second stitch and so on.

We were talking about chain circles before. We can practice the single crochet stitch with the circle. Place the crochet hook into the circle. Put the wool over the hook. Place the wool around and pull it through the two loops on your hook (we went through this before) to form a single crochet stitch. Carry on repeating the same process until you have worked all of the circle.

When you get to the other side of the circle, join the circle up by placing the hook through the first single crochet that you made, wrap the wool over the hook, and pull through both stitches on the hook. To tie off, cut off the wool and then pull it through the loop on your hook. This time, pull tight to fasten.

Double crochet

The double crochet is the second basic stitch that you need to learn. It is one of the most useful, if not *the* ultimate useful stitch in crocheting. Once you have mastered it, you can put it to use in creating sweaters, shawls, afghans, home and celebrations décor, and lots of other projects.

We start with our already worked circle.

Insert your hook into the desired stitch. Yarn over your hook (YA) and rotate the hook towards you. With the wrapped yarn, pull the hook through the stitch. At this point, you should have two (2) loops on the hook. YA again and draw the hook with the wrapped yarn into both loops on your hook.

You have now created one (1) double crochet (U.K. style). If all is OK, there should be one (1) unstitched loop on the hook. Repeat.

The double crochet is explained in different ways by different experts from different countries. More than often, there are differences even between experts from the same country. It is such a basic stitch that it cannot have a single description on how to make it. It is always better to hear different opinions to understand properly.

For example, double stitches can be explained as below from an USA expert:

"Start a new chain and join it so you are ready to try a new stitch. The double is a stitch that is little larger than a single crochet. Place hook into a circle and wind wool around hook for the commencement of the next stitch. Repeat the stitch outlined in bold above until you have a complete circle then join off the circle as before."

Two ways to explain the same thing — the fun is to find what matches you.

Treble Crochet

Continuing our journey through the main stitches, it is time to learn the treble crochet. Treble crochet is another key basic stitch that you are likely to need for a number of crochet projects. Trebles can either stand alone, or, like all other basic stitches, can be fused with other ones to make stitch patterns that are pleasing. Trebles are versatile and can be used in every way imaginable. They also work in numerous configurations, such as triangles, circles, squares, rows, and many other shapes. You can use them in almost any thread or yarn, which means you can try practically any material. No need to say that new material has to be experimented in a later stage of your learning experience.

You can begin your crocheting from a starting chain. Alternatively, there are many ways you can get started. We will consider the start of our work from a chain for now.

Instructions:

Your chain should be 3 more chains than the number of triple stitches the pattern needs.

Skip the first 4 chains — they are turning chains. Your hook is already through the single loop you have in your chain. YA twice. Insert the hook from the front to the back of the work into the center of the fifth chain (having skipped four, remember?). YO through the chain. You should have four loops on your hook now (see image below).

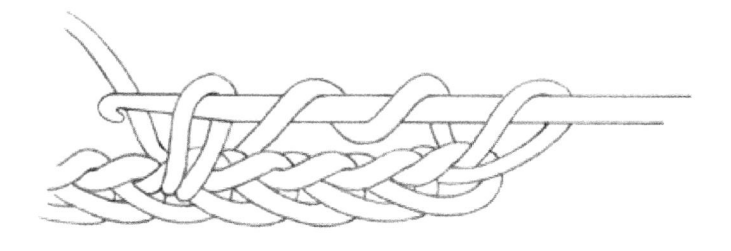

YO and draw it through the two loops currently on the hook (3 loops still on the hook). YO and draw it through two loops on hook (2 loops remaining on hook). Yarn over, draw yarn through the remaining loops on the hook and you've completed one triple crochet (see image below).

One treble crochet

YO twice, insert the hook into the middle of the next stitch, YO, and draw it through the stitch (YO, draw through hoops on hook) 3 times. Repeat until you get to the end of the chain. Now you are ready to begin the second row.

To begin, you must turn your work. Start by chaining four (turning chain). Skip the first treble (we talked about it in the beginning). YO twice. On the next triple crochet, insert the hook from the front to the back under the top 2 loops and repeat 3 times. Your first triple crochet now done. Repeat this step in each treble until you reach the end.

The image below shows what your work should look like when you are working on a flat item rather than a rounded one.

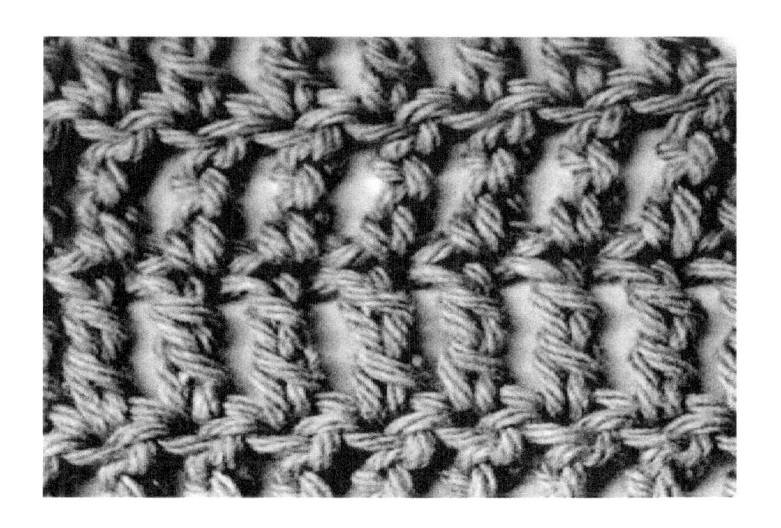

Treble crochet

Learn to Crochet a Granny Square

To make your first granny square is an experience you will not easily forget because making your first granny square opens up the craft to so many possibilities. The funny thing is that most of the instructions you can find around on the web are about how to make hats, scarves, bags, and all sort of pieces you can make using your crochet skill using granny squares as base. However, it is somehow difficult to find how to make a granny square itself as a complete beginner. If you are beginning to crochet, you are beginning to research about crocheting too. Now, considering that everyone wants to start from the beginning and not from the middle, we will fill this gap together.

To start, we will make a slip knot and chain four (4) stitches. We went through slip knots and chains before. Please have another look at the instructions so you will not be disappointed in making a mistake in something that you previously knew how to do. Bear in mind that the first quality you must develop in crocheting is not patience (which is the second one) but finding the way to not get bored while practicing as beginner. Training is boring only if you skip one passage of it before. This is the rule that can be applied for every sport, hobby, or profession.

Instructions (we start with the simplest way from the very beginning):

Make a slip knot. Put your hook into the knot and chain four (4) stitches. Put your hook into the first stitch on your work.

YO and pull your yarn through. On the loop on the hook, slip your stitch through.

This is the famous "ring center" (center of the granny square), which is actually your best friend at this stage. At the center, the hole is where you'll do everything that consists of the first round.

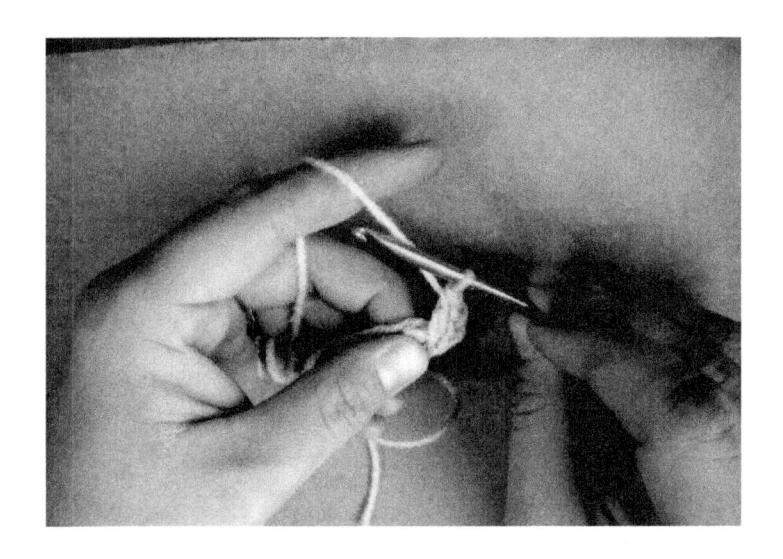

Double crochet in the center ring

Chain three (3) stitches and double crochet into the center ring, repeat, double crochet again.

Now we arrive to the "shell" concept. The "shell" is made up of three double crochets. You've just made the first shell of a granny square. The "chain three (3)" replaces a double crochet. In the first round, it will be a series of four shells and you will chain two (2) stitches between each shell.

Make another shell by chaining 2 and making 3

double crochets (this is shell number 2). Repeat the above (this is shell number 3).

Make the last shell by chaining 2. You should have 4 shells. You can now join them together.

Chain 2 stitches and put your hook into the second stitch of the first shell.

YO and pull through, making sure your hook is through the stitch. Now slip stitch.

The first round is now done. All of the rest of your rounds are just a repeat of this one. What differs is the number of shells you make and how many chain stitches between them.

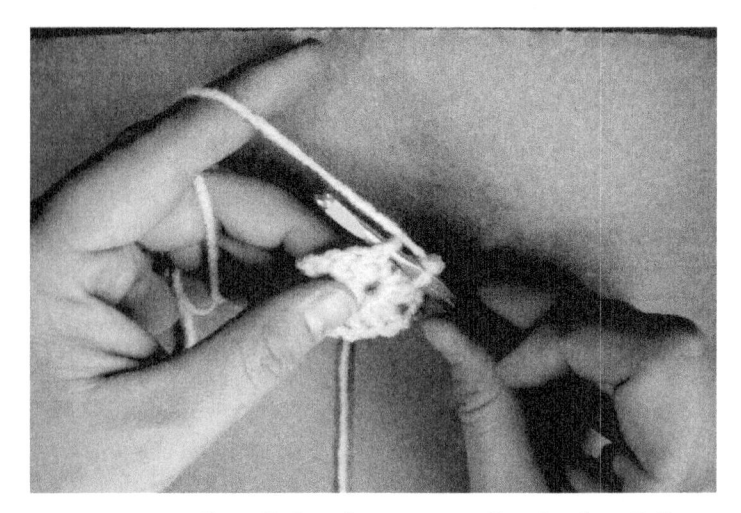

Put your hook in the second stitch of the first shell.

You now have 4 shells, ready for joining together.

Chain 2 stitches. Put the hook into the second stitch of the first shell (image above, the second stitch on the chain three we did after making the ring).

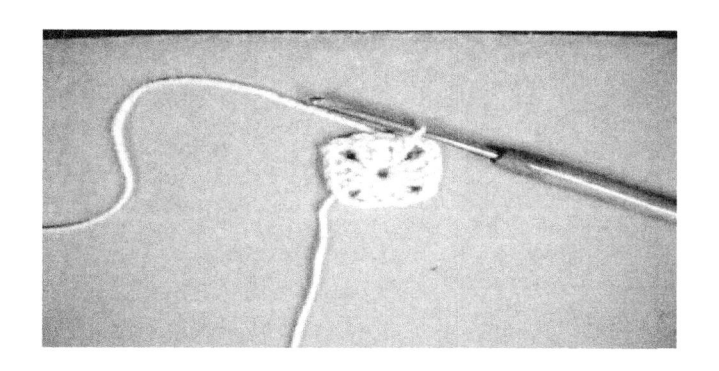

First round

Granny square

Of course, the granny square explained is one color only, but I guarantee that when on a table and people know that YOU made it, they will ask you to make some for themselves.

If you are confident enough, you may want to try a multi-colored granny square. If so, try to follow the project below.

To make the multi-colored granny square, you will need scraps of wool in at least three colors as this project is for three colors. Make a chain of six chain stitches and join into a circle. Make two more chains. Work three trebles into the hole in the center of your circle. Work three chains to form the corner. Work three chains to form the corner.

Now in sequence:

Work three trebles into the same central hole.

Work three chains to form the corner.

Work three trebles in central hole.

Work three trebles in central hole.

Work three chains to form the corner.

On the last side, work two trebles and then join to the first treble that you made by placing the crochet hook into the first set of chains that you made, thus creating a square. Cut the wool, pull it through the loop, and pull it so that it is firmly tied off.

In the next row, just use another color. Make a loop in the wool and pull it through one of the corner holes in your small square. Make two chains, work two trebles in the corner hole, and then work three chains to form the corner. Each corner is worked the same way. Continue, and when you are satisfied, put the hook through the beginning of that row. Pull the wool through the beginning of that row and pull it to finish the row. You can continue forever actually.

Next color: Two chains to start the row, and then three trebles, three chains, three trebles in corner holes and three trebles on their own in all other holes around the square.

How to put granny squares together

To crochet them, hold one against another (right sides). Work under the outside loops only. The first square (top) should be a little bit farther than the bottom one. Put your hook through the outside loop nearest you then the one farthest from you. Then put the hook through the outside loops of the corner of the stitches and pull through both loops (image below).

In the next two outside loops, put your hook through and YO. Pull your yarn through and make a slip stitch chain. Progress through your work, slip stitching all of the stitches (make sure you're only using the outside loops).

If you want to join more than two squares together, don't fasten off.

Add Stitches of Interest

So we learned the basic stitches and the granny square. We can now learn more stitches that may be shown on the crochet patterns to make it beyond pretty and elegant — a little plus to extending your abilities as a crochet. The scallop is one of the most popular among those stitches. It is versatile and very effective as an edge, and is used to create interesting designs.

Working a scallop border

You do not necessarily want to work in a circle now. Maybe you want to work on something using backward and forward crocheting. The scallop border is the best to start with. The scallop border is also known as shell edging too, as it is formed in the same way as the crochet shell stitch (we went through shell stitches before).

Basically, a scallop or shell is formed by working several stitches in one base, forming a shell, semicircle (that would be a more correct term actually), or scallop shape as you can see in the image below.

To work the scallop, you need to know single, double, treble crochet, and slip stitch (this should not be a problem for you now). There are literally hundreds of ways and uses for a scallop border. We will make one simple example, considering what you've learned so far by reading this guide.

Make a loop and work 30 chains

Work a double crochet into the second chain along and carry on making double crochets until you reach the end. Turn the work and work another row of double crochets in the other direction. If you build up four rows, this will be sufficient to work a scallop border around. Cast off your wool by putting the wool over the hook, cutting the thread, and then pulling it through, fastening neatly.

Start in the middle side of your "oblong". The idea is that you work a scallop pattern all the way around. Make a loop in your new color (remember, we are using more than one). Pull this through your work with the crochet hook.

Work six double crochets so that your semicircle of stitches lies flat, then work one single crochet through the piece that you are finishing off with a border. This creates one scallop.

Make two chains. Work six double crochets into the work at about the same distance, creating your second scallop, and so on. When you arrive at the corner, you will be able to work a scallop using 12 double crochets instead of 6. After that, carry on along the other side with the sets of six double crochets forming the scallops.

The corner

For sure, you already understood how many combinations you can create using this formula.

Besides, if you browse the internet, you will find a lot of people who sell scallop borders for good money. So scallop stitches can be a business too. For someone out there, it is already. Think about it.

There are literally thousands of different variations that you can use to make your crochet work interesting. This is the beauty of crochet and knitting — the only limit is your imagination. Once you experiment a little with different stitches, you will find that you have patterns that you prefer and you will pick up the ones you like as you go along; for example, edging a towel using scallops or simply use single crochet to edge a wool blanket.

Try edging something using your skills. You can find numerous links on the web teaching you ways of using what you've learned so far with a great repertoire of possibilities. You can make handbags just by using a nice picture. The best way to do it is by using knitting patterns. You put the design into a grid and you simply count the rows and stitches and you can place the pattern where you want it to appear.

Using Different Stitches to Their Best Advantages

The best way to get accustomed to the different stitches you have learned is to make a sampler. You can begin with a chain of whatever length you like. The most common and more typical are chains of 25 links for a small sampler, but it is totally up to you.

Create a chain and then work one row of double crochet stitches. Turn the work around and work another row of double crochet stitches, then trebles for two rows. Follow this with working into every third hole and creating three trebles into one hole before working on the next third hole to make your next group of trebles. Trebles are very suitable for grouping work. You can try different block groupings.

Do two rows for all the designs that you decide to

experiment with. This provides you with a clearer image of what you can produce using that particular stitch. You can always refer to your sampler when you are making something if you need to verify how you achieved something. Most experts create samplers in multi-colored wool so they can clearly see the stitches. It takes a little longer, but it's worth the time.

Typical sampler

Decreasing and increasing
When you make garment, you will need to decrease and increase to make the shape of the pieces that form the garment. As usual in crochet,

what you have to do is much easier than you might imagine.

To increase a crochet, just increase the stitches in the same hole, which makes the current row have more stitches than the last.

Decreasing is done by working as shown in the diagram below. The image is better than the description. However, it is worth it to spend some time describing how to decrease.

To decrease in crochet, you the pattern normally but omit the last part of the stitch, leaving the worked loops on your hook. You then work the next stich as usual, with the last stitch's loop still on your hook. At the end, you pull your hook through all of the loops to combine them together.

Although you might consider the above as very complex, it actually isn't. As most of the other stitches, it is easier to do it than to explain how to do it. It is just a combination of stitches you learned in the beginning of the book.

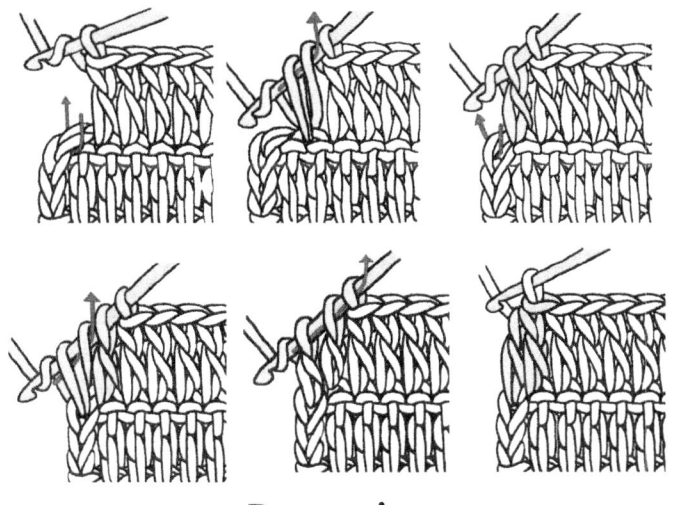

Decreasing

Edging work

Where you would have used blanket stitch in normal embroidery, try chording an edge. The way of edging work is done in a simple manner: by using double crochet. But you've learned different stitches, so use your imagination and do not stick with the easiest one. Maybe you can do a better job using your skills and the stitches you already know, surprising yourself with the results. All your friends will be amazed too.

Trying your hand at using crochet cotton

You knew we were going to end up talking about cotton. Honestly, who does not want to try to crochet cotton if he or she likes the art of crochet? As soon as you get more experienced, you will run to your shop and invest in a little cotton crochet and a much narrower size of hook.

Of course is worthwhile to experiment with different thread thickness and also with different crochet hook sizes.

I would like to remind you that crocheting is not only a practical skill, but it also has a part that deals with collection too. In other words, you will often buy materials and hooks only because they are beautiful. You will likely have your set of colors and materials (not to mention different hooks), even if at the end of the day, you will only use the "old good ones" you love most. Of course, your favorite shop keeper will be able to tell you which hook would be the best to use in conjunction with your choice of thread. But still, it is a matter of love. You can choose one less comfortable just because you like it. It is *your* hobby, after all.

Glossary of crochet abbreviations

To read crochet patterns, you will have to memorize a lot of abbreviations or have detailed glossaries at hand. This is not a problem. On the web, you can find many in different languages. The best suggestion at this point is to stick to simple patterns. If you cannot understand the abbreviations, it is very likely that you did not master crocheting enough to create that particular project. It is a good idea to create your own glossary too, with the abbreviations you want and use most, including those that your brain does not want to memorize.

Crochet abbreviations:

SC - Single crochet

DC - Double crochet

TR - Treble crochet

YO – Yarn over

CL – Cluster

WS and ***RS*** tell you whether you should be working on the "wrong" side or the "right side".

CH – Chain link

This is all basic. Most patterns have glossaries included, which show you what all the abbreviations mean, so do not be worried about them.

Classic and Less Common Crocheted Artefacts

After these basic instructions, you will be able to enjoy crocheting and spending your spare time doing something you really like. You can add a little bit of fantasy and vintage to your house and make your parties and celebrations unique with your crochet works.

As I told you before, Christmas can be different and your friends will definitely praise you for your Christmas tree full of joyful angels, shining balls, and stars. Your little presents will be unexpected and useful. Can you imagine what it means to open a gift box and discover that someone spent the time and used their hands to make the most original Christmas gifts? It is amazing and emotional! I suggest for you to free your mind and realize your ideas. Sometimes, we do not trust ourselves and minimize our possibilities. But if our imagination and eccentric projects come out, they will surprise us.

Of course, to have a mentor at the beginning will be easy and reassuring, encouraging you to reach a goal. For this reason, I will continue to offer you suggestions. I started with Christmas and I will continue from this important celebration.

Apart from the Christmas tree, you will enrich your table for your family celebration meal with lots of beautiful things you can do with crochet. Coasters and matching napkin holders can be an addition to your Christmas table, together with a centerpiece and chair cushions. Choose your favorite color between the tradition white, red, and green and create your personal decorations.

Do not forget that you have to welcome people and there is no Christmas door without a Christmas wreath!

If you have children, every year, you have to find a surprise for their Epiphany Day.

Why do not hang Epiphany socks full of candies, sweets, and goodies? Epiphany socks are a good introduction to the everyday objects section. It would be a long list and different from one person to another. I will suggest mine and I hope you can add lots of yours to it.

Let's start with the blanket. Sooner or later, everyone needs to possess a warm, colorful handmade crocheted blanket. It would cost a lot of money or a lot of time if you decide to make it yourself.

A beautiful crocheted afghan with granny squares of approximately 40"x 60" can cost around 100 Euros!

Another reason to start? It can be considered a Zen practice in many people's opinions, not just mine. Some people are impatient, hate wasting time, and are extremely stressed about life. Many of them find their path to Zen in some wool and a stick. Some of them are creative, but they do not know how to express the color of their souls. Crochet is a chance for them — you only need a hook and a ball of yarn and you will feel total wellbeing very soon. Once you've finished, you can enjoy snuggling on the couch or lay on the lawn. Be proud, as this is your milestone.

But what else can you make and use in everyday home life? Lots of things: a hanging basket, storage basket, potholder, bathmat, shopping bag...Do not forget personal things like wallets, pencil cases, keychains, glasses cases, mobile cases, and purses.

Beautiful vintage purses

Fashion on the Catwalks and in Shopping Centers

Last, but not least, is the use of crocheted artifacts in ready-to-wear clothing and haute couture.

Unlike knitting, the art of crochet has never become fully mechanized, so in ready-to-wear clothing, it's never become popular. However, it is a versatile technique whose applications have ranged from everyday life to haute couture.

If crochet were to become more mechanized, its potential is enormous when it comes to clothing and fashion.

The popularity of crochet hit a peak between 1910 and 1920 with Edwardian fashion. However, it was in the 1960s that crochet was transformed from the intricate work of the Edwardians into the bright colors and granny squares which appealed to the psychedelic youth and emerging hippie culture. In the '70s, its popularity grew with dresses, coats, jackets, and so on, being made in a variety of shapes and colors.

Nowadays, all these items are gaining popularity once again, and are gracing our fashion catwalks, appealing to all those who crave expression of the hippie laidback bohemian vibe. Especially now, true vintage crochet dresses and capes, ponchos, coats have become the most sought after items in musical and entertainment shows. Crochet is warm, sexy, versatile, unique, and so bohemian. Seen on many celebrities and models, crochet is a beautiful look for many occasions — in whites and creams, it is a terrific look for a wedding or bridesmaid's dress if you like bohemian, gypsy, or hippie-looking weddings.

When Mary Quant started her revolution designing the miniskirt, the garment symbol of the '60s, she was already known as a designer. She did two collections of knitting and crochet patterns for

Courtelle in 1965 and 1966. The Mary Quant patterns were stylish and fashionable: who could forget Jane Birkin in 1969 in the Emilio Pucci crochet gown?

Pucci, together with Gucci, Ralph Lauren, and Dior, designed amazing crochet dresses worn and made famous by unforgettable actresses and singers of those years, such as Bridget Bardot, Sylvie Vartan, Catherine Deneuve, and Audrey Hepburn.

Recently, fashion designers have revived crochet dresses, skirts, hats, and more in their recent collections on the catwalk, recognizing its popularity, beauty, and versatility.

Many celebrities and models have been seen in a variety of crochet items, especially maxi dresses for red carpet events. Crochet pieces have, of course, hippie inspirations, but today, the aesthetic is always luxurious.

This popularity of crochet is not only a prerogative

of haute couture, but even of street fashion. You can easily find something vintage and easy to wear in many shops all other the world.

Early Origins and History

We do not know many things regarding the early origins of crochet because the ancient textiles that survived are very few. Some claim that originally, women used fingers to create loops and chains.

Only later did they begin to use a tool very similar to the current hook, which was initially made of wood, bone, or bamboo and then in ivory and amber.

The oldest find, considered a precursor of crochet, comes from Jutland. It is a woolen cap that dates back to about 3100 years ago. However, primitive textile samples were found in every corner of the globe — Far East, Asia, North and South America, and Europe.

Some scholars believe that Tambour work was at the origin of modern crochet. This technique was used in China. It required the use of a fine hook to weave threads through a netted background.

This technique arrived in France around 1720.

An American scholar, Mary Thomas, believes that crochet work originally comes from the Arabian Peninsula. From here it spread eastward, in Tibet, and to the west, in Spain and then, thanks to merchants and sailors, even in other parts of the world.

The most delicate crochet form originated in Italy in the 16th century and was used by the sisters for making ornaments and vestments. It was considered a typical occupation within the monasteries where sisters created precious lace using very thin yarns. The linen for the altars were fitted with crocheted borders not only for decorative purposes, but also to make it more durable. Very soon, it spread to Spain and Ireland, which were very Catholic countries.

Only in the 19th century did crochet begin to be

appreciated in the bourgeoisie and the noble. The laces were used to adorn the linen of the house and underwear. Lace, finished with precious scallops full of picots and various decorations, had a huge development especially among the ladies of the bourgeoisie, and they adorned their precious clothes with collars, gaskets and tippets.

The crochet, which until then was not considered a genre in its own right, developed to mimic the difficult points of Venetian lace. The work was faster than needle and bobbin lace and tools were simpler and easier to find.

Perhaps its popularity took off from a lady of French origin, Eleanore Riego de la Branchadière, who settled in Ireland, where she remained impressed by the delicacy of the work of the nuns in a convent in Dublin. She not only perfected their skills, but spoke of the art of crochet in her magazine "The Needle". She also published eleven books in which contained conversion tables from needle lace and bobbin lace to crochet.

She is commonly credited with the invention of the Irish Lace. When times were hard, women had to find ways of supporting their families. This was particularly true during and after the great potato famine of the 1840s, when crochet became the sole economic support. Another factor that contributed to the spread of crochet was the creation of a kind of domestic industry born in Clones to help the poorest families, thanks to Cassandra Hand, the wife of a local parish priest. The Clones Lace, still widely known, is a variant of Venetian lace. The Venetian lace, although very beautiful, required considerable time and Irish women found that by using the crochet hook, they could achieve the same effect in less time. These women reproduced elements linked to their environment: shamrocks, fern, brambles, wild roses, daisies, or star-shaped figures.

When Queen Victoria promoted the crochet lace in an exhibition of Arts in London, fashion took off. Soon, demand became so high that professional sellers took the place of charities and the activity of lace turned from survival activities into an industry. The patterns of crocheted lace began to be written and distributed. Irish girls traveled to other parts of the world to teach crocheted lace.

From the Irish Lace came the Orvieto lace, which, over the years, has acquired a peculiarity and original identity. In 1907, the Ars Wetana, a "patronage for young workers" was born. It sought to carry out the activity of production and packaging of lace and frill with special ornamental details for the Duomo of Orvieto, aimed at strengthening and development of local crafts.

The popularity of crochet reached its peak between 1910 and 1920, with fashion of the Edwardian era. Its models were more complex stitches and the prevalence of white yarn. They began to be printed in series books with crochet patterns that took the place of honor in the decoration and creation of clothes and household items.

In 1930, fashion acquired simpler features. Art Deco was the trend of the moment, and crochet was used primarily for garments of children and infants, christening gowns, gloves, and blankets. During the Second World War, yarn was rationed and since crocheting wastes more yarn than knitting, crochet seemed to be doomed.

Despite the fact that crochet was all the rage in Europe, it hadn't really gained much popularity in America. The majority of women who crocheted were immigrants who loved the availability of ready-made threads and other materials.

After the turn of the century, America finally accepted crochet and it became part of the many skills taught to young girls. It was considered a leisure activity since it did not produce a functional or marketable good. It was pretty much reserved for the middle and upper classes.

In the '60's/crochet came back strongly in vogue after long hibernation, using the vivid colors of granny squares.

Crochet's popularity continued to grow until the '70's, with ponchos being the must-have accessories.

In the '80's, crochet began to fall out of favor. The economy was growing and more women were working, thus having less time for crafts. Plus, crochet work was no longer affordable.

Crochet and knitting lost their importance even in the school curriculum — nobody taught it anymore, and the new generation had no time to learn. This time, it seemed that crochet was really facing extinction.

Fortunately, since the middle of the '90s, crochet has experienced a new period of interest. Crochet can be seen today as a hobby, but for those who have awareness, they consider it an art form.

Beginner's Designs Tutorial

Baby Bib

A baby bib can save your baby's clothes from stains and also help you reduce the clothes that need laundry. It's not a secret that kids love to play with food, so it is important to minimize the probability of getting it on the baby's clothing. There are a lot of bibs for babies in stores and you can buy whichever you like or create your own baby bib in this crochet pattern guide.

What you need:

Different colors of yarn

Crochet hook no.2

Begin with making a chain of 30 loops. Knitting will be made in both directions with single crochets.

In the next 9 rows add one loop on both sides.

Change the color white to gray and knit three rows with single crochets.

Change the color to white again and knit number 22 rows with single crochets.

Further, we skip one loop on one side and make 11

row with this pattern. We turn around the knitting, skip one loop and knit till the end with the single crochet

Then we decrease the number of loop only from the right side and skip in each second row one last loop.

The same work is done on the other side. Decrease the loops from the left side.

Tie around the bib with yarn.

ELLEN WARREN

And we get such a beautiful bib for a little boy. To make the same bib for a girl, just change the yarn colors to pink and red

A Crochet Baby Bib

Little Turtle

Little Turtle Crochet is an unusual souvenir or a toy for your baby. It is made of natural materials.

Prepare for work:

- Cotton yarn (light green and bright light green color)

A hook with a diameter of 1 mm

Material to fill the toy.

The main color of the product is green. Start with 8 chains

1st row - tie a chain with the 5 single crochet and knit first and last loops 5 times.

2nd row - knit the same way and knit the

central loop 5 times.

3rd row - knit without changing the number of loops.

4th row - knit the central loop 3 times.

5th row - knit 2 loops at each end with the single crochet three times.

6th row - knit without changing the number of loops. The first part is ready.

Knit another part with the same pattern.

In a second part knit 2 rows without changing the number of loops

Now connect 2 parts with the green thread and fill the toy with the chosen material.

Then knit 4 small circles and sew them. It will be the legs.

For the head make a knot and 6 chains.

1st row - knit each loop twice.

2nd and 3rd row - knit without any changes.

4th row - skip every third loop

Fill the head.

Knit one more row unchanged and sew the head to the torso.

ELLEN WARREN

Sew the eyes and, viola! Your turtle is finished!

Little Toy Turtle

Snowflakes

To induce a New Year's mood, everyone must feel the holiday from the decorations of the house. The various thematic handicrafts, including snowflakes, help get everyone in high spirits. We will show how to make a snowflake with crochet with detailed description of the scheme for beginners. The approximate diameter of the snowflakes is 8-10 cm.

For knitting you need:

- thin white yarn

- the hook (1 mm).

Begin with the knot.

Tie it around with a 10 single crochets. Next, knit according to the scheme described below:

1st row number - make 2 turning chains and then two chains more

Now knit a double crochet in the loop, locate the next one in the circle.

Make 2 chains again.

2nd row - knit 3 double crochet in each existing gap between the columns. Double crochet from the previous row knit with a double crochet.

3rd row - make 2 double crochets and then make 7 chains. Finish the raw

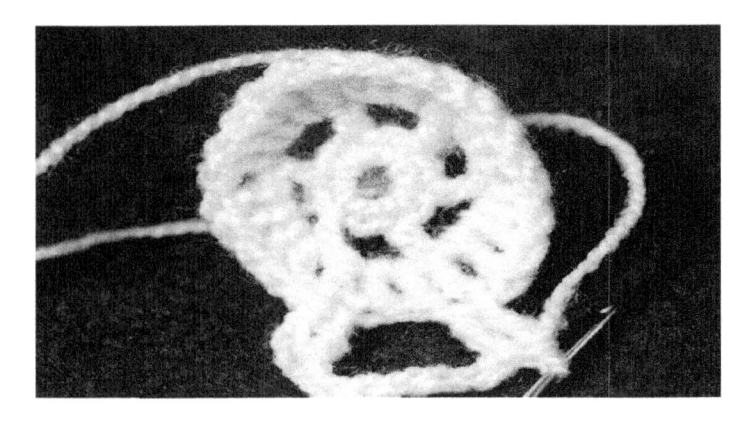

4th row - make a chain. Knit 4 double crochets in the middle loop. Make one more chain and then knit 4 double crochets. One more chain

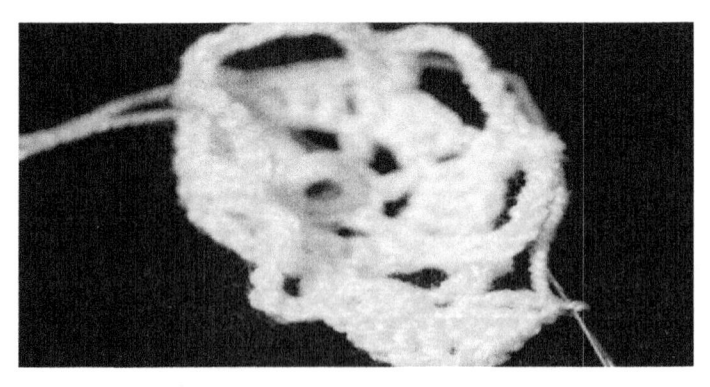

5th row - knit three chains.

In the gap between the existing columns you knit 4 double crochets, 1 chain and then 4 double crochets again.

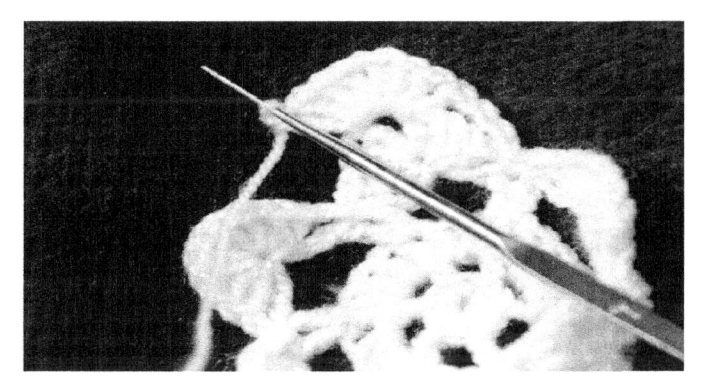

Make three chains. Close the row.

6th row - make 5 chains and one double crochet. Now do the knobs - knit three ordinary chains and finish in the first loop.

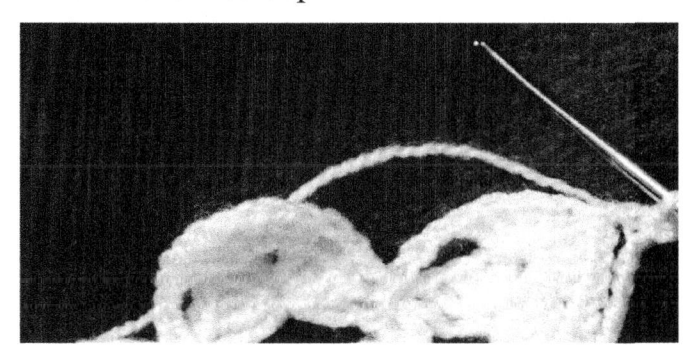

Then knit two more double crochets and make another knob

Make the last double crochet, one chain, another knob and the chain.

Knit the second part of the element symmetrical

Then knit the circle and the snowflake is ready!

Snowflakes, New Year's Handicrafts Decoration

Crochet Potholder (Single Crochet)

Making a potholder and crocheting the pattern in this guide is an achievement to every beginner in the hobby of crocheting. What's good about this potholder guide is that you will be crocheting something that has practical use in the kitchen. In this guide, you will practice making the last and also the first stich in one row of a single crochet. I hope you enjoy this guide!

What you need

Balls of cotton (Varying colors depending on your preference)

Crochet hook (size 9 – 5.5mm is best)

Instructions

Start with the ball of cotton with the color that you prefer to be inside. After this, chain 31

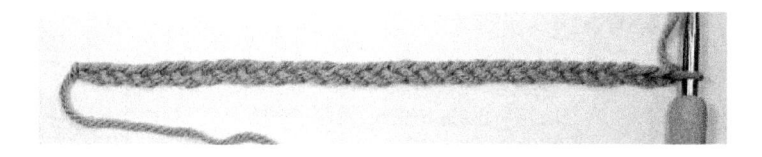

1st row: Simply crochet into chain and in the second chain, start using single crochet until you reach the end of the row (which is 30 stitches).

2nd row: After, just chain 1. Turn your crochet the other way to start the second row. It may help you to mark the number of stitches on a piece of paper so that you would not lose count while stitching.

Pick up two loops on top of those stitches, and then simply single crochet again (30 stitches). Once you reach the end, you have now finished the 2nd row. Keep track of the count to avoid any errors in the process.

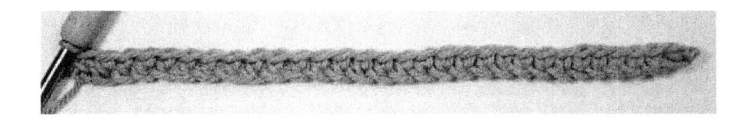

3rd – 30th row: After the end of each row, simply chain 1, turn the crochet around and apply single crochet until the end of the row (30 stitches), keep count!

Repeat these instructions until you have finished the 30th row. It should look something like the picture below.

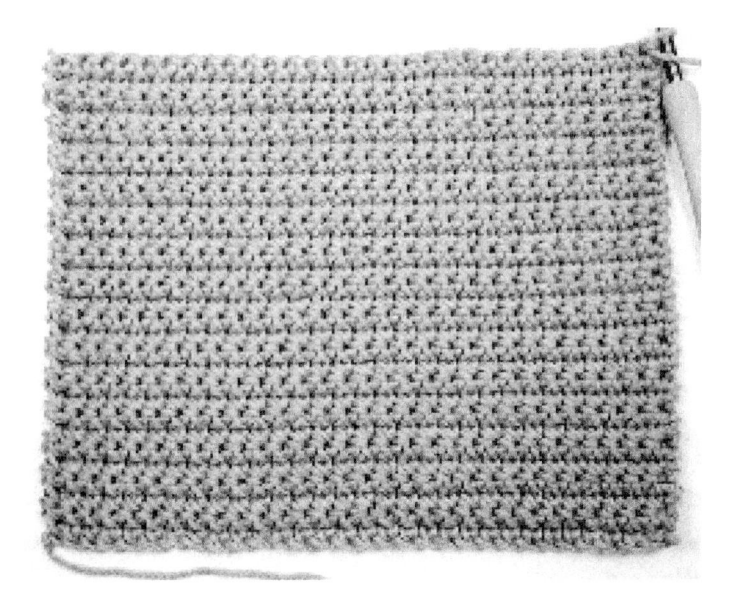

After finishing the 30th stitch, cut the end of the yarn (at least 4 inch allowance) then pull it through the last loop at the end of the row. Make sure to pull it tight enough and secure it with a knot. (Binding off)

Repeat all the instructions at the top and create another one. (Check the picture above) Use the other color that you picked, by the way. This side is the outer part of the potholder. But remember not to cut the end of the yarn on this second attempt.

In attaching these two pieces, you would need to create the other one having its rows side wards and the other one up and down. This is an IMPORTANT step in the whole guide. If you do not follow this correctly, you would not be able to create a potholder.

It should look something like the picture above. The back piece is the last one you have created and the one on top is the first one that you made. Make sure that your crochet hook is properly placed like on the picture above.

On the back piece, chain 1 and do not turn the crochet around. Observe the picture below. After you have chained 1 you should put it through the two square layers. See the picture below.

The picture below shows how you should put it through the two layers

Remember that your hook should be placed between the stiches in the first row for security. A more secure crochet results from this

After crocheting the loose ends for 4-6 stiches it is time to pull it a little to secure the whole row.

Make sure not to pull it too tightly though

Slowly crochet along the edges of the squares. Be precise in stitching one layer to another row. Just slowly bring the two squares together. You can also count the number of stitches from time to time and compare it to the rows. Make sure that you have not missed a single stitch in the process.

When you get to the corner, single crochet 3 times to create stitches on the same corner. This would allow you to properly place your crochet hook and allow it to move to the next side. Keep going on the other side and pick up row by row and stitch by stitch until the end. Repeat the process.

At the picture below, it shows loose ends (2, in fact). Simply go around both by single crocheting around 4-6 stitches. Pull the short end to make the whole structure secure. Don't forget to push the end between the two square layers. Keep going until the last loose end and repeat the process of single crocheting 4-6 stitches and pulling to secure.

Now on the third side, repeat the process of single crochet 3 around the corner and continue to the last side.

Single crochet then chain 6 more stitches and skip 2 stitches which would then lead to you slip stitching into the third one.

Now it's time to cut the yarn. Make sure to create

an allowance of at least 3 inches and pull it through the ending loop. Pull it and create a knot, making sure that it's secured well.

Hiding the thread that remains is easy. Simply put your crochet hook at the top and pull it inside to hide it. Make sure that it ends up inside the two square layers.

Congratulations! You have now created your own crochet potholder. You can use this to hold your pot and other hot utensils used for cooking since it has a very heat resistant property that would prevent you from burning.

Little fish for children

Children are very fond of different toys with unusual textures. In addition, these products develop imagination and motor skills, which is essential for the first years of life. In the master class a detailed scheme is shown below:

For this fish we need:
- natural yarn (orange and white colors)
- hook (1 millimeter diameter)
- some wool yarn.

Start with making a loop with orange thread and tied it. Then knit 8 single crochets.

Bring up the knitting in the ordinary circle and pull it together hard enough.

Next, knit according to the scheme:

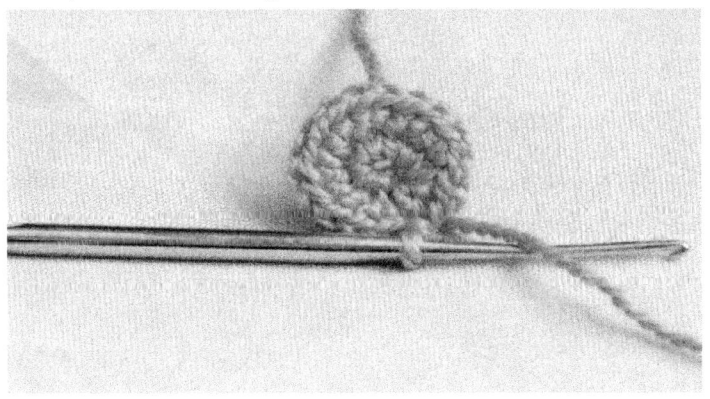

1st row - knit each loop twice.

2nd row - knit similarly without changes.

3rd row - knit every second loop twice.

4th row - knit without changes.

5th row - change the thread to the white one. Do not change the number of loops.

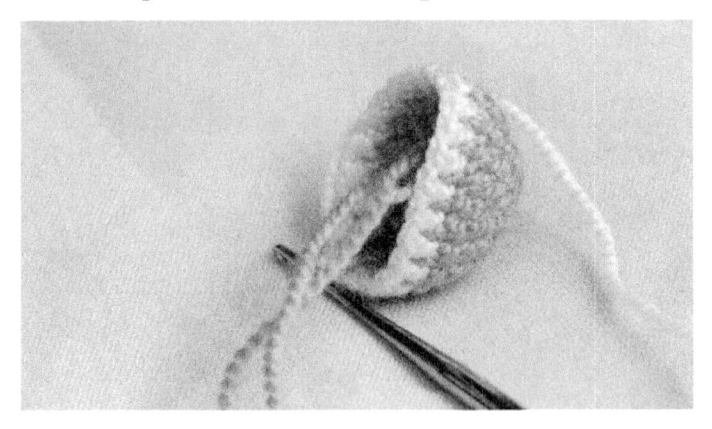

6th and 7th row - now go back to orange thread and knit 2 row with it.

8th row - knit the first 3 loops with orange thread. Then next 4 loops you need to do with white thread. And finish the remaining 3 loops with orange thread. Absolutely symmetrical knit the second half of the row.

9th row - knit with the white thread.

10th row - reduce every third loop.

At this stage you need to fill the toy with some wool yarn.

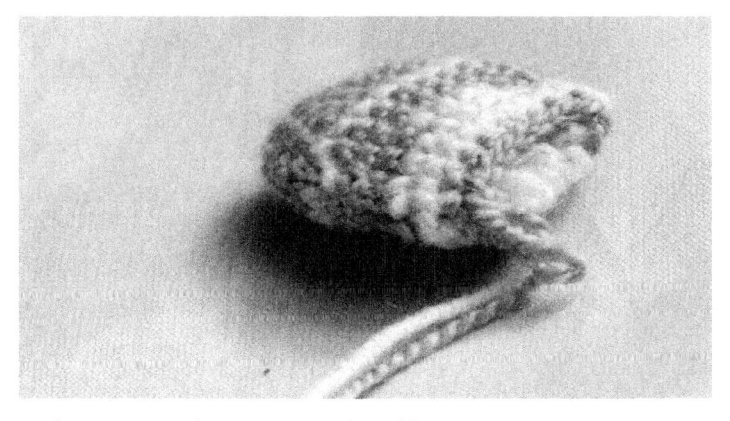

11th row - reduce every third loop.

12th row - reduce every third loop again.

13th row - knit without changing the number of loops.

14th row - switch the color to orange and knit without changing the number of loops.

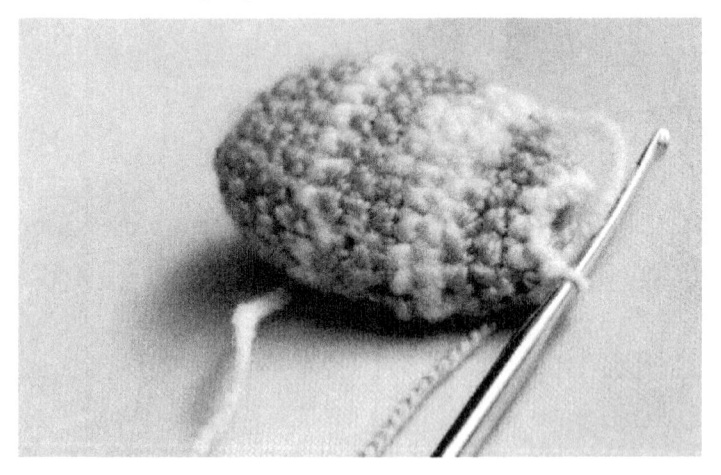

And finally, we come to the tail. Pull the edge at one side and knit

7 double treble crochets.

To knit the fin we catch a loop near the head and knit treble crochets along the back.

ELLEN WARREN

Than sew the eyes and the toy is ready! Knitted

A Stand for the cup

One of the main and most popular elements of crochet is a circle, which is the basis for a variety of products

In order to make the usual flat circle with the single crochet make the knot first.

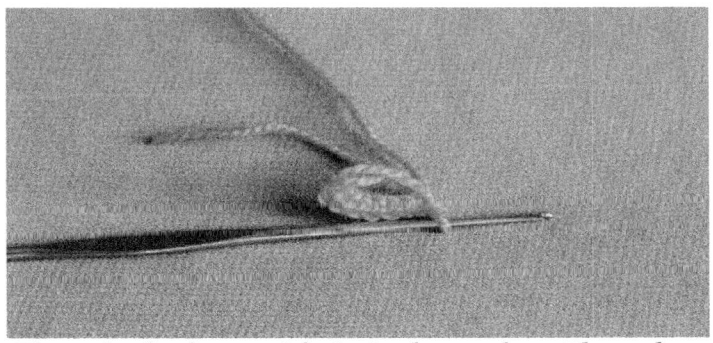

Then tie the knot with 8 single crochet. Then close

the circle and pull tight the free thread.

Now knit as described on the following scheme:

1st row - knit each loop twice. Close the circle

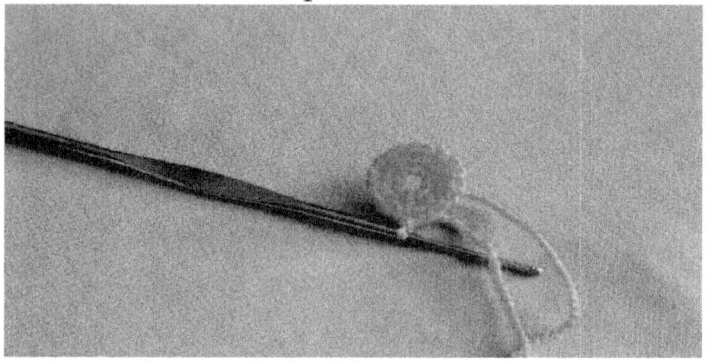

2nd row - knit each third loop twice.
3rd row - knit the same way as the second row.

4th row - knit without changing the number of loops

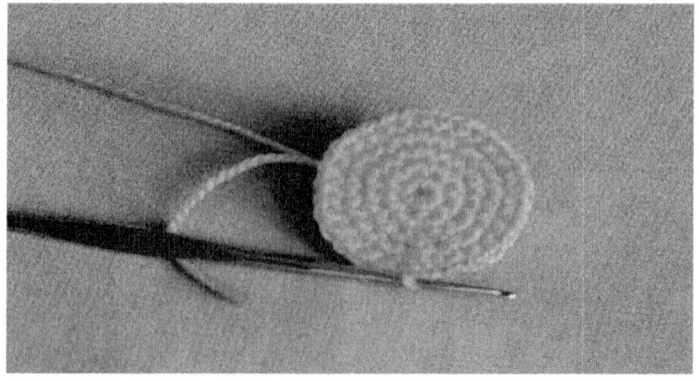

5th row - knit as always twice every third loop.

6th row - knit circle with any changes.

7th row - knit every 5th loop twice in a row

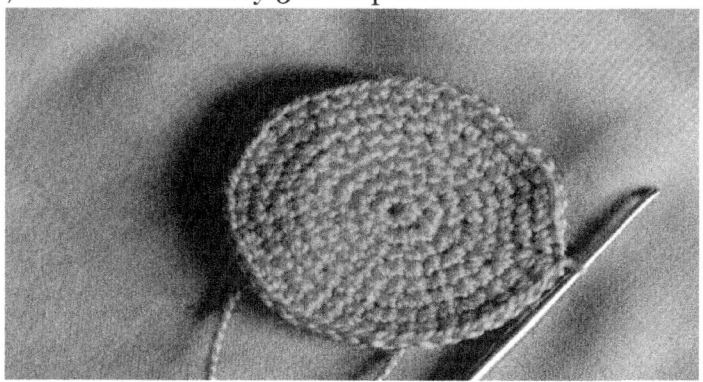

8th row - perform exactly the same as the previous one. Then tie the product with a white thread without changing the number of loops

It is a simple product and it can become the great stand for a hot cup.

Cabled Coffee Cozy

This is something any beginner can create easily as a first project. Wrap your mug with this cabled coffee cozy for more comfort and temperature resistance. If you want to try creating this eco-friendly alternative, continue with the following steps.

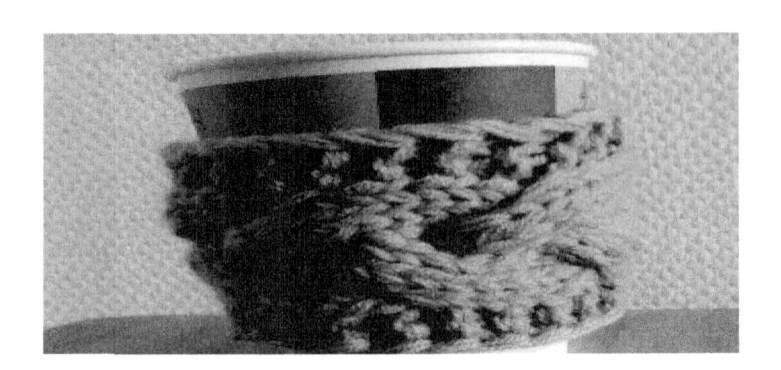

This is something any beginner can create easily as a first project. Wrap your mug with this cabled coffee cozy for more comfort and temperature resistance. If you want to try creating this eco-friendly alternative, continue with the following steps.

What you need:

Yarn (50% wool-mohair yarn is a pretty good pick)
DPNs (Size 10, if available)
Mug/tumbler

How to make your own cabled coffee cozy:

1. To begin creating your own cable coffee cozy, make sure to cast 32 stitches. Avoid moving it in a way that may cause the cast to twist.

2. Pattern the yarn around 3 times (or more depending on your judgment). It is ideal to form 12 rows in the process for a more secure covering.
3. The next step after patterning the yarn is to bind off. Make sure that you do this a bit loosely and not that tight.

Shape your cabled coffee cozy using your mug/tumbler. And viola, you have now created a cabled coffee cozy that you can use every day.

Little Angel

A wonderful decoration for a Christmas tree will be a little angel. How to make such an unusual decoration?

What need to work:

- yarn (2 colors). The main color should be white, and the second may be gold, silver or blue. - a hook (1 mm diameter) - material to fill the toy.

Start knitting with the head of an angel. Take a white thread then make a loop.

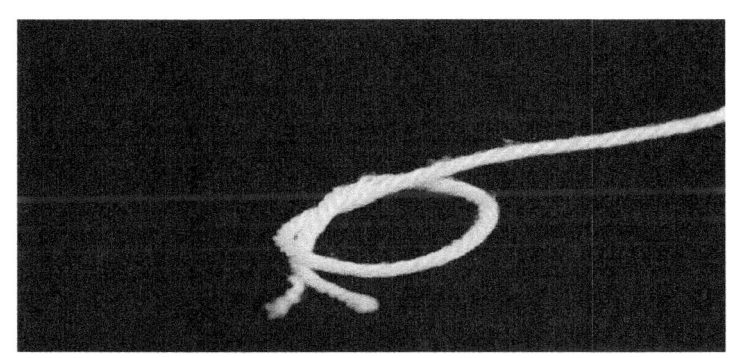

Tie the loop with the 8 single crochets.

In the second row knit each loop twice with a single crochet.

3rd row - knit the loop twice, but only every third

loop.

Then knit 3 rows without changing the number of loops

Now slowly begin to diminish the circle - reduce every fourth loop.

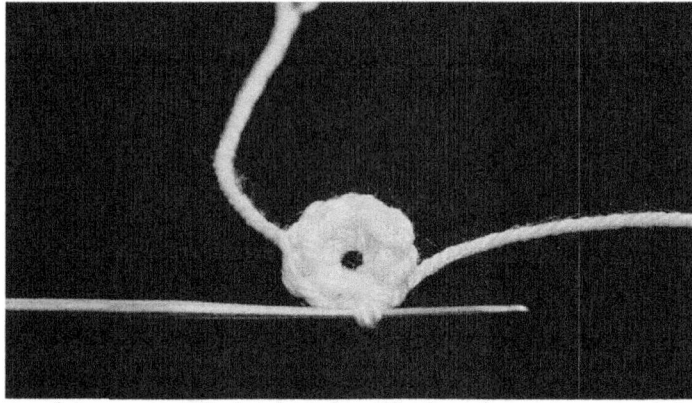

At this stage fill the head with the chosen material.

Within the next two rows of knitting you have to

leave a circle with six loops.

Then knit 2 rounds without changing the number of loops.

Now we are getting to the dress.

1st row - knit each loop twice with a double crochet

2nd row - knit every first loop twice with a double crochet and miss every second loop.

3rd row - knit every second loop three times and miss every first loop.

4th-5th rows – Simply repeat the pattern.

The following 2 rows knit as follows - knit each loop four times with the double crochet. Your angel's dress is now ready.

Take a different color thread and tie it to the edge of the dress.

Now it's time to do the halo.

Knit each loop three times over the head. Grab a loop near the neck and make 8 chains

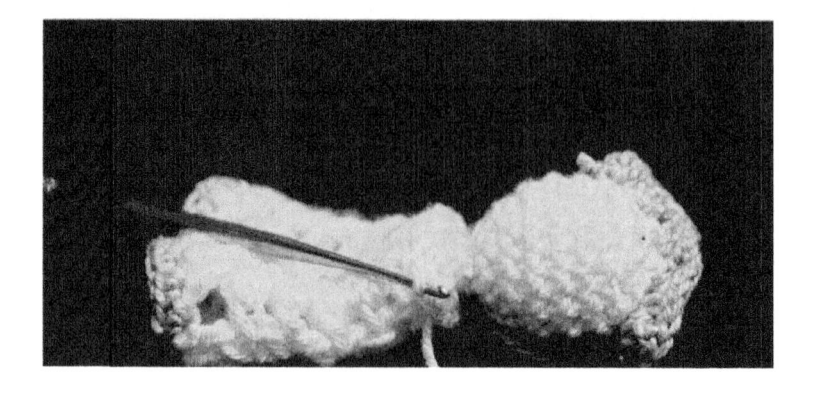

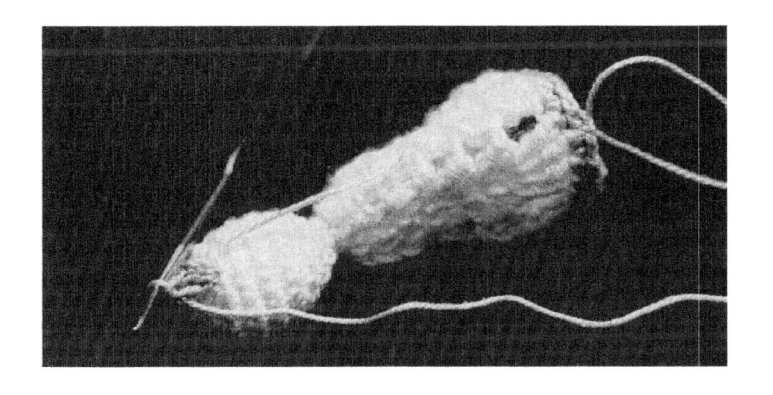

Connect the chain with the next loop in a circle. Finish the circle.

Now let's do the wings. Grab a loop and knit it with 6 double crochets. Next, take the middle loop and make 4 double crochets. Then make a chain and finish with 4 double crochets.

Do the same with the other wing.

Tie the wings around with another color.

Done!

A wonderful decoration Little Angel for a Christmas tree

Conclusion

Thank you again for downloading this book!

If you follow the instructions, this book will help you to see how easy crocheting really is. Crochet can be simple or as complex as you make it. In fact, as you get more and more experienced at crocheting, you will enjoy challenging yourself to create more and more projects. Creating crochet items is a great way of relaxing and will become second nature to you. As you practice and practice again using the images in the chapters relating to use of the crochet hook, you will soon find that this is something that you love to do and you'll work without even looking at what you are doing. It's that easy.

Why Crochet?

Because it an easy to learn hobby, you can put it in

your pocket and take it anywhere with you. Because crochet allows you to carry on your work in a moment of pause, at the bus stop, waiting for your children to come out of the school or gym. While waiting for Public transportation, you can get on, sit, and pull everything out to keep working. Because it is a therapy, great for soothing a tired and stressed out mind. Because it's a relaxing way to express your creativity and fill your life with colors.

As you work on a piece, for a while, you can forget your frustrations of the day and channel your mind into your work. Crochet is so relaxing that you will get completely lost in your new creation. When you finish for the day, your mind is refreshed.

Finally, if you enjoy reading this book, please take the time to share your thoughts and post a review on Amazon. It'd be greatly appreciated!

Thank you and good luck!

ELLEN WARREN

**** PREVIEW OTHER BOOKS BY THIS AUTHOR****

[Excerpt from the first Chapters]

"ONE DAY QUILTING MASTERY" by Erica Stewart

Introduction

When you begin to quilt, you'll be joining a longstanding folk art tradition that has a really important place in American handicrafts. While quilting didn't begin in America, it's come to symbolize a lot of the American Spirit and the ability to make beautiful art out of whatever you have on hand.

Quilting is one of the oldest folk arts still practiced today. While once quilts were made strictly for utility, as a way to keep the family warm while using up leftover scraps of fabric, today's quilts have become an art form that many people enjoy both aesthetically and for the creative process that making a quilt entails.

Quilting may seem intimidating for beginners. Often

times a quilt pattern will require you to cut what feels like countless small pieces of fabric before stitching them together just to form the quilt top. The top then has to be backed, bound, and quilted, often by hand with thousands of tiny stitches. The entire process can often be enough to make you want to give up before you've begun and start searching for readymade quilts on eBay.

I thought the same way once. Quilting can be an addiction, however, and once you begin you may not want to stop. While it's true that making a quilt from start to finish can take you months to complete, there is something peaceful and meditative about the process. Watching your quilt come together can be immensely satisfying, and the rocking, rhythmic quilt stiches you'll put into the finished quilt will become second nature before you've even finished quilting the first block.

In this book you'll learn the roots and the basics of quilting. You'll see how quilts came to be made, and why they're such an important part of women's art history. You'll also learn how they're put together and some simply patterns that you can try for yourself. When you're ready to move on, you'll also find some tips that can help you design your own patterns, creating quilts that have your own personal stamp on them.

Quilting is a handicraft, but it's also an art and quilters are artists in the way they piece together colors, patterns, and designs. Whether you decide to make a variation of a traditional pattern or you want to create something all your own, learning to quilt can be a worthwhile and satisfying endeavor to take on.

A Brief History of Quilts

Many people believe that quilting is an American art form, one that is celebrated today as being one of the most important parts of American Folk Art history. And in many ways this is correct; quilting as we know it today developed in America as a necessity. Women who didn't have access to large pieces of cloth took leftover scraps of fabric from other pieces to make bedding, designing different patterns as a way of differentiating them and decorating their homes.

There are other cultures that were quilting in their own way long before America became a country, however. Ancient Egyptians for example are the first to have joined together layers of fabric with a batting in between them, making what are thought of as the very first quilts. Hawaiians, known now for their beautiful and dramatically colored applique quilts, had a whole cloth style of quilting long before the islands became a part of the US, their current quilting style only developing after missionaries brought the piecing and appliqueing techniques of the continuous states to the islands.

The quilting stitch used to hold together layers of fabric was first used in the 11th century to form padding for men to wear under their armor when they rode off to war. Layers of fabric were joined together with what may now be thought of as basting stitches as a way to help hold the padding together longer, making it more comfortable for the men to wear. It wasn't until the 18th century, however, that this type of quilting stitch was used to hold together layers of bedding and became a needlecraft.

Quilting as a type of bedding first started in Europe and was brought to America with people looking to emigrate. These quilts had little in common with the quilts we know of today; they were whole cloth quilts of complete pieces of fabric with batting in between, quilted with decorative stitches. Large bolts of cloth were more common during this time in Europe, and scraps were given other purposes, rather than putting them together to form a larger sheet.

Quilts made of multiple pieces of fabric arranged into patterns and stitched together or quilts decorated with applique designs to become the quilt top didn't start making an appearance in a widespread way until the beginning of the 19th century. Before this, many women were beginning to piece together quilt tops from scraps of fabric, but doing so in a decorative way that could be shown off wasn't thought of yet. From there quilt patterns were designed, printed, and swapped between women as a means of creating art and warm, durable bedding from scraps of material left over from dressmaking and other household items. When flour and seed manufacturers began to print decorative designs onto their sacks as a way of appealing to women who made clothing and bedding out of the inexpensive fabric, quilting for more decorative purposes truly began to take off, with women working out ways to combine a variety of different colors in one quilt to form a cohesive pattern.

This history explains why many quilts can be found under multiple names, as well as why certain blocks can be arranged in a variety of ways; a quilt block was designed and given to a friend or neighbor who pieced the many blocks together in her own way, which didn't necessarily match the way it was first designed.

Even as quilting began to take off as a popular needlecraft, most women in more well-to-do homes had little to do with the art for many years. Until showcases such as the World Fair began to show quilts as a viable means of creating art – and not just as a way to create bedding from leftover material for those too poor to purchase whole cloth – quilting was still not considered a pastime for women of means to enjoy. Once quilting was seen as a form of art, with applique and decorative stitching begin to take the place of things like embroidery as a way of showing off a woman's skill set, it became far more popular for many more women to enjoy.

Quilting fell out of favor as a popular needlecraft and art form around the 1940s. From then until the 1970s it was considered to be passé, or something that was only done due to necessity, not something that needed to be done in an age of readymade bedding.

Quilting saw a resurgence in the 70s, however, emerging to become one of the most popular and important American folk art techniques still used today.

With the invention of computer software, quilting took another turn, with artists and quilt makers finding it easier than ever to design their own patterns, making quilting into a very much current and popular art form once again. Today, quilting is seen as a prized hobby with the hours of work that go into each quilt being given pride of place in anyone's home. It's not uncommon for quilts today to be used as wall hangings or as a decorative covering in guest bedrooms, with many quilts being considered as "too good to use".

Quilts are designed to be used, however. Even antique quilts can be prized for the wear and tear that show with loose threads and thinned fabrics, because it shows that a quilt was well loved and well used over the years. This double utility – that of being both an art form and a usable product help ensure that quilting endures to this day.

Types of Quilts

When you think of quilts, you may be imagining the type pieced together from several different scraps of fabric. This is only one type of quilt, however; there are several and each has its own attributes and history.

Whole Cloth

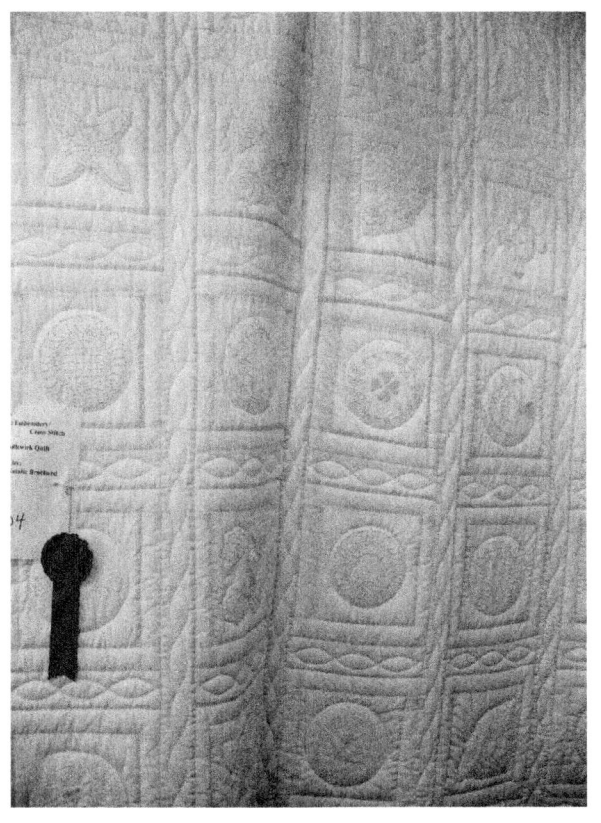

Whole cloth is one of the oldest types of quilting, and while not as popular as other quilting types, it is still practiced today. A whole cloth quilt is made up of two solid pieces of fabric with batting between them. The quilt is bound on the edges and quilted with decorative stitches and patterns. It's not uncommon for a whole cloth quilt to show off multiple types of stitching to show the skill of the artist, so a quilt may have a roll of scrolls and roses, followed by a row of waves, then by one of a design of the artist's creation. Sometimes "blocks" are stitched into the quilt with quilted borders between them to help show off the quilter's skill with a needle. It's not uncommon in this case to find that each one of the "blocks" shows a completely different pattern or image within it.

Whole cloth quilts are arguably easier to make because you don't need to spend time cutting and piecing, but because the quilting therefore becomes the focal point of the design, you're skills need to be very well developed before you take on this type of quilting. For many quilters, a whole cloth quilt is something that they take on only after years of practicing their skills on many different pieced and appliqued quilts first, and after they've had a chance to try designing their quilts as well because the finished results will require all of these techniques.

Scrap Quilts

It can be argued that any quilt made out of scrap fabric could be rightfully called a scrap quilt, but I'm using this term to specifically describe those quilts made out of squares or "scraps" of fabric that have no pattern or design to them. A true scrap quilt will be made up of multiple squares placed randomly through the quilt. The quilt may be tied, rather than quilted, meaning that instead of quilting stitches joining the three layers together, pieces of yarn or ribbon are used to tie together the layers together at regular intervals. Scrap quilts are arguably the easiest type to make, and are often made by beginners as well as children who want to learn to sew and make their own quilts.

Scrap quilts can be very beautiful in their own way, with several different variations available. One variation is known as the Postage Stamp and is made up of very small pieces of fabric, most around 2-inches in size. When seen from across the room, the finished quilt is a riot of color and pattern and can be great for brightening up any room of your house.

Pieced Quilts

Pieced quilts are made up of several different "blocks" sewn together to form the top of the quilt, which is later backed, bound, and quilted. The blocks are made up of different patterns, usually repeating so that the whole quilt forms a pattern made up of the different pieces. Some quilts, like the Log Cabin, Winding Ways, and the Tumbling Blocks pictured above are made so that individual blocks make up a bigger, overall pattern.

It is also possible to make a quilt out of multiple blocks that have nothing to do with one another. This is known as a "sampler" and it's a nice way to perfect your skills and to learn how to do progressively more difficult blocks. For example, you might start with a simple Nine Patch for your first block and eventually get to a more difficult Dresden Plate by the last one.

Pieced quilts are probably the most common, and they can be made up of many different types of fabric. You can use readymade designs for your blocks, or you can create your own.

Applique Quilts

Applique is a method of quilting that has you sew individual pieces of fabric onto a larger piece of fabric to make different and intricate designs. Some quilt patterns will use both piecing and applique to get the desired effect, while other quilts may be done with just applique. Applique patterns often use blocks the way that pieced quilts do, but you can also make some whole cloth quilts with applique patterns covering the entire surface to get a completely different look.

Applique isn't any more difficult than piecing; it's simply a different kind of look. When many people are completing their first sampler, they often include one or two applique blocks to get used to the technique at the same time as they learn to piece. Applique can add a lot of depth and richness to the finished quilt by letting you work with shapes that wouldn't be possible otherwise, so it's a very worthwhile technique to master.

Art Quilts

Art quilts are one of the newest types of quilting. They

combine piecing, applique, and whole cloth techniques with fabric painting and dying to get very unique and signature looks. Often an art quilt won't be made up of separate blocks but will instead be viewed more like a single canvas that tells a larger picture or story.

Art quilts can be among the most challenging to make, simply because there isn't a set pattern, stencil, or template you can use when creating them; you have to work out the design and ideas for yourself. The biggest difficulty in this lies in translating your ideas from a drawing or computer program onto a much larger canvas – the quilt itself. Because blocks are rarely used, you need to be able to envision the quilt as a whole, then translate that vision into the final size and form. It's like creating a very large canvas after having worked only in miniature; you need to have an appreciation for scale as well as technique before you can begin.

It's not uncommon for very accomplished quilters to try their hands at art quilts once they've mastered other techniques. It can be a way of establishing yourself as a quilter and as an artist, while expressing yourself in fabric.

Tools and Materials Needed for Quilting

No matter what type of quilting you intend to do, the type of materials that you need really isn't going to differ all that much. Quilts can be made entirely by hand, entirely by machine, or a little bit of both. Depending on how you intend to go about making your quilt, you'll need at least some of these supplies:

Fabric

Quilts can be made from anything. I have quilts made of wool, cotton, polyester, flannel, and even one that I made out of baby clothes! You'll need enough of whatever fabric you choose to piece the top, as well as solid piece for the back, and enough fabric cut on the bias to bind the edges. Use scraps, old clothes, fat quarters, old sheets, or anything you want to make your quilt. Some people even use pieces of fabric as they are, such as making a complete quilt out of old neck ties.

Pins and Needles

You'll want some basic quilting pins to hold your fabric in place before you sew it. If you intend to hand sew your top, you'll want some basic sewing needles and thread, and if you intend to hand quilt the three layers together, you'll also need some quilting needles. The larger the needle, the slower you'll go, but the easier time you'll have when starting. You may want to invest in a few sizes at first until you're comfortable.

Rotary Cutter and Mat

No matter what type of quilt you make, chances are you'll end up cutting some fabric. A rotary cutter makes this simple, as does a cutting mat. If you're cutting anything with curves, a good pair of fabric scissors is also recommended.

Quilting Frame

A quilting frame holds together the three layers tightly as you hand quilt. It's only necessary if you intend to hand quilt; you don't need one to tie or to machine quilt. Quilting frames can be very large, holding the whole quilt at once, or small enough to fit on your lap. If you have an embroidery hoop already, you can even use this to start.

Cardboard

If you're making a pieced or applique quilt that uses the same pattern pieces over and over, you'll save time by cutting out the initial shapes out of cardboard, then tracing them onto your cloth to cut. You can even save your cardboard templates to use again and again, perfect for quilts that use very basic shapes.

Graph Paper and Pencil

While not necessary, you may want some graph paper and a pencil to sketch out your quilt so you can see how your ideas will look, design your own patterns, or lay out a sampler.

Sewing Machine

You don't need a sewing machine to quilt, but it can make the process faster if you piece by machine. Any sewing machine can be used for this particular stage, even the old Singer your grandmother may have left you.

Quilting Machine

Few people have the funds to purchase these, but many fabric shops have them set up for you to rent and use on site. This allows you to quilt your three layers very quickly and easily, enabling you to finish a quilt in days rather than months.

[Excerpt from the first Chapters]

Printed in Great Britain
by Amazon